UP, DOWN, AND ALL AROUND

Life – True or False

Rosemary Szablewicz

Rosemary Szablewicz
48 Zachary Way
Mt. Arlington, NJ 07856

First North American Copyright © 2025

ISBN: 979-8-89669-083-2

DEDICATION

Bill, for his belief and patience; Jennifer and Matthew for your support; Michael, Anthony, and Isabella for being yourselves; Kathy and Georgette for your enthusiasm and Members of the Writers Workshop and Writers Forum for their encouragement

Acknowledgment

I would like to recognize those who are in the industry, and who have supported and brought me to this point of the writing process. Emma, Daniel, and last but not least, Rachel.

Thank you for your patience and sharing your knowledge.

Contents

Dedication ii

Acknowledgment iii

About the Author v

She Looked Around to See If Anything Was Taken 1

A Perfect Fantasy Day With ELVIS 3

A Scare 11

A Time I Said No 15

All Your Sorrows Will Vanish 19

Fear Of Flying (In A Plane) Conquered 21

A Memorable Haircut 25

Memory – What Memory 29

Hearing – Repeat That, Please 31

Eating an Oreo Cookie 33

The Letter Opener 36

Why Can't I Have a Cookie? 38

Dare to Cross the Line 41

SIXTY 43

About the Author

Rosemary Szablewicz (Leonard) was born and raised in Brooklyn, New York. In 1972 she and her husband, Bill, moved to Long Island to start their family. They have two children: Jennifer and Matthew, and three grandchildren: Michael, Anthony, and Isabella who complete the family.

Twenty years ago, Rosemary and Bill moved to northwest New Jersey. This change in locale enabled them to reside in closer proximity to their expanding family.

The enjoyment of writing first person essays, creative fiction, non-fiction stories and observations on whatever event or situation captivates Rosemary & mind has brought her to the point of writing her first book to share with her readers.

Rosemary has been published in various periodicals and newspapers in New York, New Jersey, and South Carolina such as Newsday, Post & Courier, Good Housekeeping, Travel Holiday, House, and the Long Island Pennysaver. She is the Moderator of two northern New Jersey library writing groups, Writers Workshop and Writers Forum. Rosemary also volunteers in her community and borough activities.

Rosemary and her husband travel extensively and reside in northwest New Jersey.

She Looked Around to See If Anything Was Taken

The cold drift of air she felt on the back of her neck prompted the wisps of her upswept hair to sway. She looked around the spacious fitting room of the elegant salon but saw no one. Nothing was taken. All was in place.

As Millicent began to undress and try on the new evening garment laying on the pink silk Louis XV chair, she sensed Raphael's presence from across the room. Their eyes met. Suddenly, it seemed as if he were standing directly in front of her. His irises, the color of coal, pierced her blue eyes. She felt as though she was looking into two black, endless orbs imploring her to meet him.

Millicent acted as though she were hypnotized. Gently, she placed the long red velvet frock she was about to purchase atop the boudoir chair in the changing room. Picking up her cloak, and under some bewitchment, she walked out of her favorite dress shop without the beautiful gown.

Her preferred tearoom was located a few doors down the avenue, and she briskly made her way there. Once inside, she was greeted with a nod by the proprietress, Nina. Taking her usual seat in the quiet corner of the 1880s cafe at the appointed table, Millicent ordered a pot of Typhoo Black, his favorite. Tea in the English porcelain teapot and freshly baked biscuits awaited as Raphael walked to their table. He effortlessly approached her and, with a casual flair, removed his black top hat and complementary cape. The heavy forest green drape hanging on the overhead rod enveloped them as he drew it closed.

As Millicent stood, her cobalt blue taffeta long skirt rustled against his body. With that, Raphael encircled his arm around her petite waist. An icy chill slithered up her spine. At that moment, she realized something was about to be taken from her. Closing her eyes, Millicent willingly succumbed to his embrace and offered Raphael her neck.

The warmth of his bite on the side of Millicent's swan-like neck was overshadowed by the coolness of Raphael's lips.

A Perfect Fantasy Day with Elvis

As I opened the mailbox to collect the day's mail, a stream of envelopes, magazines, and coupons tumbled out and landed on the ground. Picking up the soon-to-be-recycled paper that had fallen, I noticed an ordinary small white envelope addressed to me, Romy Leon, written in a flourish of loops. Not waiting until I entered my home, I immediately opened the no-return-address envelope and couldn't believe what I was reading. The correspondence was from the King of Rock and Roll, Elvis Presley. I blinked my eyes, staring at the letter in my hand, and spoke the words out loud.

With my hands shaking and breathing somewhat heavily, I read the following:

Dear Romy,

A while ago, I read your holiday essay in a local magazine about what it would be like to spend a day during the Christmas break with me at Graceland. It touched my heart deeply, and while Christmas has come and gone, as well as my birthday, I'd be honored if you accepted this invitation to share a day or two with me and a few close friends during ELVIS WEEK, August 9th through 17th, at Graceland. It surprises me that, at my age, going on the high side of 85, my fans continue to celebrate my life and music.

Although my birthday is in January, we here in Graceland feel that August, with the lack of cold and possibly snowy weather, is a more suitable month for partying. Also, being in the open air would be the best way to whoop it up without fussing about spreading any possible virus.

I will, of course, send the Lisa Marie plane to fly you to Memphis, and the Stutz Black Hawk III will be waiting to transport you to my home. There will be a room ready for you at the Guest House hotel on the Graceland property.

Can't wait to meet you,

Elvis

I wasn't exactly in a stupor, but I was close to it. Recalling seeing the interior of Graceland in various magazines, I imagined Elvis quickly walking down the Graceland entry hall staircase with gold chain necklaces jangling around his neck. Then, reality set in and burst my happy bubble. The words Artificial Intelligence slipped onto my tongue as I showed the invitation letter to my husband.

In a trance-like state, I then called the phone number, as well as emailed the address which was attached separately to the letter from Elvis. I was more than surprised when a Graceland representative answering the call authenticated the letter.

Still concerned about AI involvement, I immediately called the Guest House Hotel on the Graceland property directly and asked if my room was available earlier than scheduled. After being put on "hold," the desk attendant said it would be if approved by Mr. Presley. That was proof enough for me, as well as my husband. Graciously, I accepted the invite for a two-night visit.

As I began to stop my trembling hands, my mind started to reminisce. Although Elvis was a guest performer on a number of TV variety shows such as Milton Berle, Steve Allen, and Frank Sinatra in the mid-to-late 1950s, the Ed Sullivan 1956 TV performance takes center stage in my mind. Recalling that 8:00 pm Sunday night, I felt like a thirteen-year-old girl again from so many decades ago, seeing for the first time Elvis Presley sing, dance, and speak.

Our console (as it was called) in 1956 had a TV screen of only 10 inches. However, Elvis looked and sounded larger than life. He was, and still is, extremely handsome, tall, slim, and his smile could melt any female's heart, regardless of age.

In a flood of memories, I saw myself as a pre-teen sitting in the living room with my parents, along with my two younger sisters, watching, without parental objection, Elvis Presley achieving stardom on TV. Mom and Dad had reminisced that when they were teenagers, they listened to and swooned over the Big Band Sound and Frank Sinatra. Growing up, I vividly recollect those songs, along with all types of music always playing on our radio. Rock and Roll was my choice. Lucky me, my parents did not object.

It was thrilling seeing, in my reverie, the countless teenage girls, as well as grown women, in the Ed Sullivan Show audience screaming and crying as Elvis charismatically performed like no one had ever witnessed on television. As TV cameras scanned throughout the theater, viewers of every age were close to fainting. It was an unbelievable sight. Even teenage boys, with their new style pompadours, looked in awe at the latest rock 'n roller.

So impressed by his singing and dancing, I sat down at the kitchen table and wrote a fan letter to Elvis. Not knowing where to send it, I mailed it to Elvis Presley in the care of The Ed Sullivan Show. Sadly, I never received a response, not even a red-ink rubber-stamped "Return to Sender" on the envelope. The fan letter was probably put in the "dead letter" section of the main New York City Post Office (now known as Moynihan Hall), along with all the other thousands of letters that were likely sent after seeing Elvis sing and swivel on TV, perhaps for the first time. More than likely, no one knew where to forward the fan letters. I would mention that story to Elvis when we met at Graceland.

As arranged, on the morning of August 9th, the Lisa Marie awaited me at a private airfield in New Jersey, my home state.

Upon arriving at the Graceland estate, I was met at the door by a staff member and escorted to the patio. The party was an informal gathering, with sounds of assorted types of music being streamed. I perused the few guests, and to my total astonishment, there stood Barack Obama at the grill, checking on a couple of the famous racks of Memphis ribs. Not only was the smoky aroma causing hunger pangs in my nervous stomach, but it also reminded me of ribs I once enjoyed a few years ago at Marlowe's Ribs & Restaurant in Memphis. At that time, the restaurant provided, as a promotion, a chauffeur-driven pink Cadillac for my husband and me as transportation from our hotel to the eatery. Bringing my thoughts back to the present while standing in the Graceland backyard, I realized that so many scents and sounds can promote vivid memories.

Barack appeared at ease, chatting with the remaining members of the "Memphis Family." I gathered my confidence and walked over to the small group to introduce myself. During the conversation, I felt a presence next to me. As I turned around, I realized Elvis had joined us at the BBQ pit. Being a home-grown southern gentleman, the King immediately extended a welcome and said, "Hi Romy, I'm Elvis," as if he needed an introduction, and shook my hand.

He was a gracious host, looking at age 86, sexy as ever in slim-fitting jeans and a loose dark blue shirt that complemented his eyes. He may not have been walking quickly down the entry hall staircase, but there were two gold chains around his neck, just as I had envisioned. His fingers were adorned with a few diamond rings. Although he was a tad overweight, that did not obscure his sensuality. His full head of dark hair had natural silver streaks through the famous pompadour and sideburns, completing the Elvis look. The boyish upturned grin of a smile remained on his nearly unlined face, and when he laughed, that mischievous lilt was still detectable.

Our lunch consisted of the now-cooked excellent BBQ ribs, sweet potato fries, and peanut butter/banana pie. Elvis and Barack laughingly bowed in accepting kudos for their outstanding rib grilling. During our luncheon banter, I noticed that the sense of humor Elvis possessed was a gift not everyone is fortunate enough to have.

While enjoying our delicious food, politics entered the conversation. There's something about licking one's fingers while eating ribs that puts people at ease while discussing normally off-limits topics. I was impressed with the knowledge Elvis had of our country's issues.

On a lighter note, Elvis regaled us with stories of how, in his spirited younger days, growing up in the South, he would sneak into all-black religious revival tents and jazz/blues clubs, listening to and then playing on his guitar the particular style of bluesy music he heard. He said not only did the music inspire him, but the style of the musicians' wardrobes influenced him as well. Speaking with Elvis, I became convinced that this man, who was brought up in a dirt-poor environment, possessed a combination of understanding the differences in all races of our nation, as well as thoughts on how to help stop the continuation of hatred.

Shortly after lunch, Barack excused himself to attend another engagement. We said our goodbyes, and Barack left the premises. Elvis asked me to join him, along with a couple of band members, in the Jungle Room, which also served as a recording area in the Graceland home. I found Elvis sitting on a brown/gold sofa in the Jungle Room, playing his guitar, and I took my seat at the other end. He began using his extraordinary baritone-tenor voice, with some bass added to it, to sing a selection of well-known songs, along with beautiful gospel/spiritual melodies, such as How Great Thou Art, In the Garden, Crying in the Chapel, Saved, and, of course, If I Can Dream from his 1968 TV Comeback Special. At my request, Elvis sang Burning Love, The Wonder of You, and I Can't Help Falling in Love with You. His voice had aged well and was more powerful when singing ballads. Elvis put so much soul into his voice that I felt swept into the emotion.

While listening to the music and talking to Elvis, I noticed a glass-enclosed medal on a side table. I inquired about it, and Elvis explained that it was the Presidential Medal of Freedom, one of the two highest civilian awards in the United States. It had been awarded to him and other well-known individuals many years ago. Elvis was humbled and honored to have received the prestigious medal. I noticed that Elvis always projected gratitude for everything in his life.

The exciting day flew by. It was late in the evening, and I was exhausted. With my appreciation expressed, I mentioned to Elvis that it was time for me to leave Graceland. He smiled, his eyes twinkling, exuding unintentional sexuality, and said he enjoyed my company. Once again, he thanked me for writing a Christmas-themed story about him. Almost at that moment, the driver and limo arrived, and I was driven to the Guest House. My room was beautifully appointed, with a bouquet of summer flowers awaiting my arrival. The next day, the driver provided transportation to Beale Street for some local sightseeing, music, and shopping at the famous general store, A. Schwab.

When I returned to the Guest House at dinner time, I was hoping to meet with Elvis again to convey my appreciation for inviting me and for hosting such a relaxing and unbelievable Elvis Week luncheon. However, at the Guest House desk, there was a note waiting for me from Elvis. He apologized, saying that he had forgotten about the plans he made to spend time with Priscilla, Lisa Marie, and the grandkids. Elvis, the adored rocker, now a loving family man. I smiled and thought that was a perfect ending to a fantastic story of my perfect visit with Elvis Presley.

While on the plane returning home and reliving the past two days, I thought about the conversation during the BBQ lunch hosted by Elvis. I came to the conclusion that Elvis was able to combine his love of all types of music—Rhythm & Blues, Gospel, Country, Rock & Roll, and Ballads. All of this music appealed to his massive audience. He created his own concept, turning it into an exciting sound for the 1950s and beyond, spanning decades and even into the next century. His swiveling hips and gyrating limbs, together with his singing, delivery, good looks, and kindness, were gifts he shared with his fans. In my opinion, to this day, Elvis personifies magnetism.

When I landed at the New Jersey airport, I remembered that I didn't ask Elvis which publication he had read my Christmas article. I'll save that question, and also relate my story about the

1956 fan letter, for another perfect day visit to Graceland and lunch with Elvis Presley.

I'll definitely ask my husband, Bill, to join me.

This story is a gift to you,

my dear Reader.

A SCARE

Yesterday evening, I experienced such a fright that the need to share the incident calls out to me. And so, I give you my story.

As per my usual end-of-day routine, I walked down the three flights of stairs, which I consider a form of exercise, in our condo building to retrieve the daily mail. Delivery to our 24-unit building's letterboxes in the entry lobby is typically in the late afternoon. As I opened the inner lobby door, I felt the difference in temperature between the two vestibules. Nothing unusual about the chilliness; the 12-degree nighttime temperature in our northwestern suburb of New Jersey that evening contributed to the freezing factor. All I could think was that I couldn't wait to return to the cozy warmth of the fireplace in our upstairs apartment.

None of my neighbors were in the outer lobby. They had used their common sense to obtain their mail and packages earlier in the day, not at 9:00 pm as I was in the process of doing. With my letters in hand, I walked the short distance across the foyer floor to the callbox to enter my code and regain entry to the warmth of the second lobby. My fingers were icy and shaking as I began to press the keypad entry numerals. And at that moment, my mind went blank. I could not recall the access code to enter on the keypad.

The digits I pressed presented the message I never wanted to read—INVALID NUMBER. The mechanical red print on the 2" x 3" screen glared at me. Under my breath, I huffed and puffed, annoyed with myself for using my weaker left hand to enter the code rather than my right. Switching the packet of correspondence to my left hand, I keyed the entrance numbers, now using my dominant right hand, thinking that was the problem.

INVALID NUMBER appeared once again on the minuscule screen. This euphemism was beginning to annoy me. My inner voice began saying, *this is how IT begins*. Upon pressing various number combinations, none of which worked, sensations of cold turned into feelings of heat, and I started sweating around my neck and down my back.

Hysterical, I am not. I am the one called upon to help bring calmness to a situation. Pressing random buttons at this point certainly was not helping my circumstances. In less than five minutes, I had diagnosed myself with early-onset Alzheimer's disease or some form of brain-changing illness. Here I stood, a "woman of a certain age," considering the possibility that my competence was slipping. Thinking of friends and neighbors in my over-55 community who had or have developed memory loss over the seventeen years my husband and I have lived here did not improve my state of mind. I couldn't call my husband to come down to the lobby and open the locked door for me because I didn't have my cell phone with me! Besides, the thought of him leaving the comfort of our condo to help his "damsel in distress," only to proceed with twenty questions, did not encourage me to do so.

Suddenly, I was saddened, remembering stories from neighbors about them writing the ingress code on the arms or pinning notes to the shirts of their loved ones to assist them in recalling entry data to gain access to the security of the main vestibule.

Attempting to relax my thoughts, I began recalling articles I had read, meetings I had attended, and conversations with friends regarding memory loss. According to all the advice from knowledgeable practitioners for the booming geriatric population, I have been practicing the proper methods to keep my mind alert and active. Nonetheless, here I am, standing alone in the outer hallway of my residence on a cold, snowy mid-January evening, locked out of the safety and comfort of the inner lobby.

It had been almost five minutes, though it felt like five hours since I left our apartment. My husband wouldn't be worried, as he knows I occasionally get sidetracked with an impromptu chat with a neighbor. It seemed, however, that everyone else had already tucked themselves in for the evening on this bleak night. Perhaps, I thought, a resident would be along shortly to pick up their mail or one of the packages resting on the foyer credenza. Ordinarily, I take my cell phone with me, but for some unfathomable reason, I didn't tonight.

As the apprehension slowly cleared from my mind, I decided to walk to the lockbox and try entering one of the many code combinations shuffling in my brain. Just then, the inner door opened, and a neighbor walked out. We exchanged a few words as I grabbed the handle of the open door. I felt relief, but also fear.

Displaying composure, I listened as my neighbor shared that the holidays had not been kind to him and his wife, who had both fallen ill and dealt with COVID. Feeling the urge to use the bathroom and feigning interest, I said goodnight, wished them good health, and a Happy New Year. I pressed the elevator button to head back upstairs. Once on my designated floor, I decided to walk down the three flights of stairs to the outer lobby again. It was important to me to see if I could remember the access code.

When I entered our condo, I placed the mail on the foyer table, grabbed my cell phone, and called out to my husband, "I'll be right back."

Standing in the outer vestibule once again, I looked at the lockbox. Timidly, I pressed the buttons, hoping my memory would recall the correct code. And lo and behold, the small screen on the control box displayed the perfect words: ACCESS GRANTED. The entry code returned to me without a hitch.

And here I am, telling the tale of my brief memory lapse. After reading more articles on Alzheimer's and similar memory ailments, I've come to accept the fact that, as we age, we may experience these occasional blips in recollection. The usual suggestions follow at the end of these wellness articles: a healthy diet, adequate sleep, social interaction, and mental diversions are all useful aids.

This, of course, is all part of the aging process, especially for the senior population. I'm thankful to have reached my eighth decade of life with my husband of almost 60 years. As of now, I haven't faced any significant glitches, for which I'm grateful.

However, as I've always reminded my children and grandchildren, worrying about a situation doesn't help you solve it. If and when troubling circumstances arise, take a deep breath and start again.

Most of the time, this approach works, and the scare is gone. Most of the time.

A Time I Said No

As a recently-turned sixteen-year-old high school senior, I was invited to a fraternity winter semi-formal party. What a thrilling experience for me! Although later in the evening, it would prove not to be the encounter I had anticipated.

I knew Bob casually from my Greenpoint, Brooklyn neighborhood. He was a young sophomore at a New York City college. Polite, intelligent, kind, and nice-looking in a clean-cut way — these are the adjectives I would use to describe Bob. Not tall, as I preferred, but he was my height when I wore high-heeled pumps.

Bob had pledged his fraternity during his freshman year and became a full-fledged brother as a sophomore. With all of this in mind, I accepted his invitation to attend the winter semi-formal at his fraternity house.

I thought about what to wear, fully aware of the expense of my two younger sisters' elementary school tuition and my own high school fees. Money was scarce for frivolous purchases. I knew my parents would not deny my request for a party dress, but I didn't want to burden them.

Since my mom's youngest sister was my height and size, my aunt suggested I borrow one of her fancy evening dresses. The off-white, tone-on-tone brocade, slightly off-the-shoulder A-line dress fit me perfectly. Because it was January, my generous aunt also suggested I wear her stylish winter coat. Elated would be an understatement to describe how I felt.

The Saturday night of the fraternity celebration arrived. Bob picked me up at our family apartment, dressed in a dark blue suit and a crisp white shirt adorned with a blue/gray tie. After meeting my parents and engaging in a bit of family small talk, we departed for the party.

I remember the night was cold, but I felt warm in my borrowed overcoat. Bob, however, said he was comfortable enough just wearing his suit. Funny, the things we remember from so many years ago. Being courteous, Bob opened the door of his car for me, and off we went to his fraternity house in Manhattan.

We reached our destination and were fortunate enough to find a parking space not too far from the three-story brownstone fraternity house, which was typical of that area of the Bronx. As we approached the building, we could hear the event in full swing, with the pounding beat of rock 'n roll music emanating from the house. Opening the front door, we were unsure which was louder—the bass of the music or the voices of the guests. Nonetheless, it was a party atmosphere.

Bob asked if I wanted a drink or something to eat. Since it was our family tradition to have steak and mashed potatoes on Saturday nights (a tradition I still don't know how we afforded), I declined the food. As for the drink, and following the advice of an older friend who had suggested I only accept bottled beer, that's what I held in my hand.

Bob introduced me to his friends, and we mingled with the crowd. After about an hour of eating, drinking, talking, and dancing, the main level of the fraternity house became congested with partygoers. To escape the press of bodies, Bob, rather than shouting, whispered in my ear, "Did I want to see the other two floors of the building?" My response was a hesitant "yes."

We walked upstairs to the second floor, which, upon looking at the number of closed doors, I assumed consisted of four bedrooms. After Bob knocked on a door and was answered with "occupied," we walked up to the third floor. Of the three rooms on this level, one appeared empty. I walked over to the open doorway and saw only a double bed covered with a mishmash of blankets and coats.

While standing at the doorway, in a matter of seconds, Bob put his arm around my waist. Literally, the tiny hairs on the back of my neck began to rise, and I can honestly say I heard the proverbial little voice in my head say, "leave." I wiggled out of Bob's embrace and said, "I'm feeling sick to my stomach, and I'd like to go home now." He offered to get me a glass of water or a Coke while he took the bottle of beer I was still holding out of my hand. I replied, "No, thank you." Bob suggested I lie down on the bed, and again I replied, "No, please call me a cab."

This happened in the latter part of the winter of 1960, and the sexual revolution was beginning to bud and blossom, but I wasn't. To Bob's credit, he was not forceful or insistent. We calmly walked down the two flights of stairs and maneuvered our way through a haze of smoke. My coat was somehow, somewhere retrieved. We walked around the sitting, lounging, and standing mass of revelers and walked out the front door.

Without a word spoken between us, Bob drove me home. Upon getting out of the car, I said good night and never saw or heard from him again.

When I climbed the stairs to our third-floor railroad flat apartment, I began trembling. I stood outside the door until the shaking stopped, opened the door, and walked into the warmth and safety of our family dwelling. My mom, waiting up for me, appeared surprised, looked at the kitchen wall clock, and asked why I was home so early. It was 10:00 p.m. I replied, "I felt ill and wanted to get home." She asked if I was okay. I said, "Yes." We said good night, and I went to bed.

So many years have passed, and we're now in another century where opinions on sex have dramatically changed. Bob did not force me into an unpleasant predicament. It remains a woman's right to say "no" at any point in a situation.

Nevertheless, at times I wonder to myself, what if I had not said "no" to Bob that night at my first college fraternity party?

ALL YOUR SORROWS WILL VANISH

Upon predicting that all your sorrows will vanish, one might assume an omnipotent being will deliver this grand news. Perhaps a prognosticator, while forecasting the future of the universe, will announce that life's slate will be wiped clean, and we will all begin anew.

Will this be a general declaration made to the inhabitants of the world, or a revelation to an individual? In either scenario, the question, "Why is this gift to be bestowed?" must be answered.

On the surface, the human race has not done well in coexisting. The endless list of wrongdoings is proof, demonstrating an apparent lack of empathy and appreciation toward mankind. Wars have been fought in the name of religion, when in reality, the cause is often the desire for power. The hatred between races appears to be, in most cases, the underlying cause of murder. Greed and jealousy are rampant. The limitless recitation of these grievances across the centuries is monotonous, with no end in sight. For a visionary, at this time, there may be no demand to erase sorrows for the world at large. Sadly, it would appear neither feasible nor acceptable to the combatant factions.

However, a benevolent supreme being has the ability to diminish despondency. A compassionate essence is kind and tolerant. Hence, if an individual or group is truly repentant for the hurtful acts committed upon members of the human race, feelings of desolation could disappear—not by the snap of fingers or the wave of an arm. We would be asked to demonstrate acts of kindness, to speak in a compassionate manner, and to smile. All of these deeds have the ability to stimulate heartfelt feelings in living beings.

Nevertheless, atonement must be made by the offender for the actions perpetrated. In retrospect, the absence of sorrow could be achieved through forgiveness. And that can only be attained if the physically or mentally injured party deigns to forgive.

Throughout the history of our planet, peaceful collaboration between mankind has been almost nonexistent. Despair, like contentment, is part of life. Allow grief to evaporate. Use heartache as a tool to overcome hopelessness. Arrive at the end of the tunnel of misery—not in a state of euphoria, perhaps, but in a feeling of warmth, empathy, and compassion.

Make the world better.

Fear Of Flying (In A Plane) Conquered

Fear of flying. No, I am not referring to the 1973 Erica Jong novel of the same three words. Although reading her book at this stage of my life would be a combination of a chuckle and a yawn. Sorry, I did not plan on the digression. However, I find writing does bring out that inclination. To digress.

I am the conquistadora of my claustrophobia, which caused fear of flying for me. In all our years of marriage, we always reveled in, and continue to do so, traveling afar. Using the airplane as transportation was a necessary, as well as exciting, part of our trips. And I was okay with the mode of transport until, on one occasion, I was not.

We were flying to the West Coast of Florida when suddenly, I felt the need to get off the plane, which was thousands of miles high in the air. The heat from my toes began to rise through my legs, torso, hands, arms, neck, and finally head. Sweating in an uncomfortable bind is not ordinarily a body reaction for me, but at that moment, I could feel the drops of perspiration on my forehead, as well as the back of my neck.

Tapping my husband's right shoulder (he was sitting on the aisle), I said, "Get up, I have to get off this plane." Bill, my husband, chuckled and said, "Don't be silly." Obviously, I thought, he was blind to my beads of sweat. I repeated, "I have to leave this plane." The woman sitting in the end seat across the aisle looked frightened and probably questioned what did I know about this airplane that was amiss. Recognizing something was uncharacteristic in my actions, Bill stood up, stepped into the passageway, while I walked to the rear of the crowded plane.

Two flight attendants at different stations stopped me on my jaunt to the restroom and asked if I was alright and if I wanted a cup of water. Although airplane lavatories are large enough to accommodate a tiny person, and less by today's cost-conscious standards, I felt relieved stretching my arms to the sides with my fingertips touching the walls of the restroom as I did. This calmed the feeling of anxiety. After patting my face with water from the sink faucet, I felt composed. Walking slowly back to my seat, I smiled at the attendants, who I am certain knew I was experiencing a panic attack. Upon switching seats with Bill, I relaxed for the remainder of the flight.

This is not the end of my story. A few months later, when off to another destination, I had the claustrophobic experience again, flying to and returning home. Upon traveling the third time in the same year, and getting anxious while at the airport waiting for our flight to be announced and embark on another getaway, we stopped at the bar lounge, and I had a couple of vodka shots to unwind before boarding the aircraft. This strategy was becoming a routine. I realized I needed help.

When we returned home from that trip, I looked for a therapist who could assist me in conquering the claustrophobia that was causing my fear of flying. I found a treatment center located in a nearby hospital, which, through my research, treated those who suffered from anxiety disorders. Having never been in therapy, I was unaware of how to navigate through this experience.

As I remember the setting, there were about ten women in the analysis circle. I listened to each woman explaining their awful, heart-breaking life situations. When it was my turn to express my fear, I felt foolish. My reason for being in therapy was so that I could handle my distress and continue to travel. The purpose seemed trite. The kind women in my group were enduring abuse, addiction, various mental illnesses, and needed help to live a fairly normal life. Again, I considered my reason, and it seemed trivial. I expressed my concerns to the group. They respectfully listened. Each woman commented and pointed out that my fear of tiny spaces was very real and would affect my life if I did not overcome it or at least learn how to cope using dependable methods. They, along with the therapist, most certainly agreed that using vodka to soothe me and risk becoming an alcoholic was at the top of the "do not use" list.

While relating various claustrophobic experiences, one participant asked, "What do you feel like doing when you are overwhelmed by the closed-in sensation? Are you afraid the plane will crash or of dying?" I answered, "No." Another group participant added, "What are you afraid of?" I replied, "I feel like screaming and am afraid of embarrassing myself." The gal questioning me looked at me and said, "Dearie, nobody ever died of embarrassment. Go ahead and scream if it makes you feel better." Looking at her truly concerned face, and with a very clear understanding, I said, "Thank you."

It is essential to say, all this occurred before September 11, 2001 (9/11). At that time, worrying about terrorists was not part of our daily thoughts. Also, in today's world, if I began screaming, an air marshal would quickly descend upon me and scramble me to the airplane floor, and my picture would be in the Star Ledger or on the front page of the Daily News. And, let us not forget about the pandemonium I would be causing among the many passengers wanting to tie me to my seat in order for them to arrive at their destination.

Years have passed, and I have come a long way since my first panic attack and fear of flying. Learning breathing techniques to control my neurosis has been the most helpful. If I am on a long flight, I stand up and walk to the lavatory. As a bonus, this stretch can prevent DVT. Without the use of alcohol, my fear of flying has been conquered, which, in actuality, was brought on by the claustrophobia disorder. It is not easy. However, compared to the variety of disorders experienced by the human population, I am in control.

When I feel the hot sensation creeping up from the ends of my toes to the upper part of my head, I recall my visits to that support group at Stony Brook University over 40 years ago. I picture the endearing woman of that caring group while I was describing my burning body temperature and how I wanted to scream at the top of my lungs, and she saying to me, "Dearie, nobody ever died of embarrassment." Although I do not practice running down the plane aisle or shrieking, just hearing her voice, while meditatively breathing, comforts me.

I am delighted to report that since my first unpleasant airborne experience many decades ago, Bill and I have traveled abroad and stateside on numerous occasions.

Fear of flying has not prevented this conquistadora from appreciating touring the countries, states, and islands of our changing world.

A Memorable Haircut

I remember the incident as if it occurred yesterday, not 40 years ago.

Planning a family trip is always exciting. However, being a working mom—whether inside or outside the home—there always seems to be never enough time. This is especially true when organizing a Disney World vacation.

For two weeks prior to our excursion, I complained daily to anyone in our household (this amounted to two adults and two children) that our youngest child was in need of a haircut. My usual hairdresser was on unexpected sick leave, and I was reluctant to make an appointment with a stylist at another salon. My husband volunteered to take our son to his barber, but I quickly remembered the last time he took our seven-year-old son to the barbershop. Consequently, I swiftly declined my husband's offer. A crew/buzz cut was out of the question.

However, at dinner that night, my husband offered to take care of the cutting problem the next day after school. He promised he would make certain Joseph would receive his usual style. I relented and replied, "Great, one less job to do."

By 3:00 p.m. the next afternoon, the work day was off the tracks. My after-school sitter called me at work to say she had to go home because her mom was ill. My husband phoned to inform me he would be home at 4:30 rather than our agreed-upon 4:00 p.m. time.

Although my ten-year-old daughter was capable and trustworthy, I felt uneasy leaving my kids for the half hour it would take my husband to arrive home from work. My next-door neighbors were unavailable to help with caring for the kids. I immediately left the office to return home. Traffic was heavy, so the preconceived quick drive turned into a three-quarters-of-an-hour journey. Keep in mind that this event occurred on the cusp of the cell phone age. Therefore, calling home while on the road was not possible.

My son's haircut appointment was out of the picture. It was Friday, and the hairdresser did not work on weekends. Almost home, I took a deep breath and said to myself, "All will work out." I must admit, I was not-so-silently saying a prayer that all was fine at home.

As I drove up the driveway of my house, everything appeared calm. Entering through the garage and opening the door to the family room, I heard the TV. However, it all seemed too quiet. Suddenly, I heard footsteps from the second floor of our split-level home.

In the blink of an eye, there was my daughter standing in front of me with a smile on her pretty face and a sparkle in her eyes. "Mom," she said, hugging me, "close your eyes." Nervously, I asked, "Where's your brother? Is everything okay?" "Yes," she replied, "and please close your eyes." In the interim of a few seconds, I heard my two children stirring and whispering.

I was about ready to open my eyes when my daughter announced that I could do so. Upon doing as she requested, there stood my son before me with his brand-new hairdo, sporting pointy bangs. His latest hairstyle was courtesy of his sister.

"Flabbergasted" is the only descriptive word I can use to describe my feelings at that moment. Actually, with my mouth wide open, no words came out for a second or two.

Still in shock, I looked at Clarissa and Joseph. They looked at me with glowing faces, indicating how proud they were of themselves. At that moment, I wanted to scream, "What did you do?" but I couldn't scold them yet for taking scissors in hand.

They said, "Mommy, now you don't have to worry about bringing Joseph to get a haircut. We helped you out." They went on to explain that they didn't cause a mess. They put newspaper on the kitchen floor with a chair on the paper, put a towel around Joseph so his cut hair would fall on it, and explained they were very careful using the scissors.

By this time, my husband arrived home. Upon seeing Joseph's hair, he was stunned as well, but thankful, as I was, that there were no accidents or injuries to our children.

Perhaps, as you're reading this tale of a hairstyle, visions of Joseph's new bob are swirling in your head. I must be honest and admit, Clarissa did a decent job cutting and shaping Joseph's very dark brown hair with auburn streaks. He did look cute. The bangs were shorter than usual with a small pointy fringe across his forehead. My husband and I asked if he liked his new cut, and Joseph replied, "Yes. Now we can go to Disney World." Clarissa was very proud of herself.

After talking to our dear children about our concern regarding the use of large scissors, and them nodding in agreement, we all went to Friendly's for a family dinner. This gave us the opportunity to discuss with the kids that although what they did was thoughtful in helping us, it was not safe for them to handle a sharp instrument, especially in close proximity to the face. We explained further that, though they were careful, physically, their strength and dexterity had not yet reached their peak.

Our children understood what the consequences might have been. Had Clarissa's hand slipped, it could have caused a severe accidental injury to both of them. No punishment was implemented for the haircutting deed because Clarissa and Joseph understood the dangerous possibilities that could have occurred.

The next day, we left for a very happy week at Disney World. Joseph sported a new hairstyle, Clarissa gleamed with confidence, and the two parents were full of pride for their offspring.

Memory – What Memory

I hate it! I absolutely go bonkers when I cannot recall a word, phrase, name, place—everything and anything.

It is frustrating; I truly want to scream. However, that is useless because it only further impacts my thoughts, resulting in a complete loss of a comprehensible sentence flow.

Obviously, my first thought is that I am losing my ability to think and remember words, places, people, and events. You know the sensation, especially as one ages. The feeling of losing a grip on life is... there I go again, reaching for a word. What would you have said?

Eventually, the comment or idea does return to me, but not quickly enough to make a cognizant statement or write my thoughts in a comprehensive manner. The declarations just escape me. They expire as I expel a breath. Anger is what I feel as the terms drift away.

Articles on dementia, Lewy body disease, and aphasia, in addition to all the signs of losing one's mental ability, fill my files on this dreaded malady. Medications to cope or slow down the process may exist, but there is no cure. Why be blessed with a longer life if one is unaware of the experiences of life or unable to recognize the loved ones surrounding them?

I am upset that dementia will rob my soul of its life.

As I mentioned earlier, the misplaced words eventually return, but the search for them in the rolodex of my brain has depleted my enthusiasm. My motivation, at this moment, to continue and expound on my opinions slips away.

Dramatic, yes, that's the word I was searching for. Take a breath. Now that feels better. Tomorrow is another day.

Hearing – Repeat That, Please

Have you recently said that phrase? Perhaps too often.

Certainly, my understanding reader has experienced this condition. Is it a condition?

A sounding board and a nodding of the head is what I am offering to you.

Added to the memory loss situation is the distress of hearing failure.

In the past ten years, I have noticed my hearing gradually slip away.

Facetiously, I would place the blame on the shoulders of BRUCE—Springsteen, that is. In 1985, my husband and I attended a concert of Bruce Springsteen and the E Street Band and sat up close and personal to the stage. The huge speakers blasting the live performance of the music from the Born in the USA album tour left me unable to hear for two days. Obviously, Bruce Springsteen and his band members are not to blame, because I chose to attend the sold-out show and sit five rows back from the platform.

Jumping many years forward, upon visiting a hearing specialist approximately eight years ago regarding my hearing deficit, I mentioned the concert I attended back in the mid-1980s. The specialist suggested that my close proximity to the speakers could have caused the hearing damage. It would appear we do pay the price when we are careless with our health in our younger, immature years.

Since that visit to the audiologist, I have become accustomed to wearing hearing aids. Nevertheless, the ability to legitimately hear is rapidly fading.

Well, that was then, and this is now, friend. Perhaps a cochlear implant will be my next aid in hearing and responding to conversations. Research, which I am now engaged in, on the implant and cost will be my next endeavor.

Between fading memory recall and hearing gaps in conversations, my vim and vigor for living are exhausting. However, I will do all that is necessary to maintain my health in all areas of my body and mind to encourage me to "keep on truckin'."

Eating an Oreo Cookie

To the uninitiated, the look and taste of an Oreo confection require a brief description. An Oreo is a sandwich cookie consisting of two small disks, each imprinted with the name "OREO," with a sweet vanilla cream filling in the center.

Over the years, the Nabisco company has produced a variety of sometimes tasty, unique-flavored, cream-filled wafers, some of which have been met with disapproval by long-standing customers. However, the most well-known and beloved version remains the classic chocolate cookie with vanilla cream filling. It is widely regarded as the best-selling cookie in the United States.

Truth be told, the Oreo is not my favorite, but as a child, on the rare occasion I indulged in one, I developed a method for eating it—making one wafer feel like two.

Sitting at the kitchen table, I would take an Oreo out of the cellophane package, hold it carefully in both hands, and twist the two cookies counter-clockwise until one came unstuck from the cream in the middle. At that time in my young life, I reveled in eating the cookie without the cream after dunking it in my glass of milk. Afterward, I would enjoy the second chocolate disk, with the remaining cream spread on it (lucky me!). I'd lick the cream once or twice, then bite into the cookie—a delectable treat. Making each Oreo delicacy last for three small bites while carefully handling it without crumbling in my hands felt like an act of dexterity.

To comprehend the Oreo-eating methods of some of my friends was a puzzlement.

Carolyn would gobble the entire cookie in two bites.

Mary Margaret, my best friend, would lick all the cream off one disk, place it in the trash, then eat the leftover disk, which had none of the thin white cream on it.

Bobby would scrape off the cream with his upper two front teeth, then shove both Oreo cookie disks into his mouth.

Billy would devour the entire Oreo in one bite.

Rita was very dainty in her manner of holding the wafer, taking tiny bites of the entire unseparated Oreo. After chewing and swallowing the treat, she would pick up any small remaining crumbs with her milk-moistened pointer finger and lick them off.

Joey would take the Oreo and toss it back and forth in his hands as if it were a small ball, until it softened, and then toss it in his mouth.

However, the one notable mental image I hold dear to my heart is of my son as a toddler eating his Oreo. As an exacting child, his evening snack request, along with a glass of milk, was two — not one or three — but two Oreo cookies, which he ate one bite at a time until finished.

Well, that is my narrative on how my son, childhood friends, and I ate Oreo cookies. Recalling these descriptive memories of the various methods of eating Oreos is probably the reason an Oreo hasn't passed my lips in quite a few decades.

It may be the best-selling cookie in the U.S., but it is not my cookie of choice. To everyone else, enjoy your OREO.

THE LETTER OPENER

Although I was cautious, my husband became anxious when I used the medium-sized serrated steak knife to open our mail. I found it especially useful for slitting open the packing tape on the ubiquitous packages from online shopping conglomerates with the "A" initial.

You may be wondering why I was using a steak knife to open letters and such. Or perhaps you agree with me that you, too, use a similar kitchen utensil for this task. The just-right size of the utility steak knife makes it perfect for the job. However, to ease my husband's worry, I promised I would be on the lookout for a letter opener.

Shortly after that conversation, while on vacation and sightseeing in Hannibal, Missouri — the home of Mark Twain — my husband and I strolled up and down Main Street, visiting charming gift shops. But no letter openers were to be found. When we inquired with the shopkeepers about paper-cutting openers, they replied no. However, they commented that such desk accessories should be available. Hmm, perhaps an ambitious proprietor will redesign the plain letter opener. One with Mark Twain's likeness would make a terrific souvenir.

I have digressed too long on the subject of letter openers, but I will end my story on a joyful note.

An individual can feel a sense of bliss at any time for anything meaningful to them. For example, recently, when I came to the breakfast table, there beside my bowl of cereal was a somewhat narrow, about 12-inch common shipping box with the usual smiling "A" on it, addressed to me. I asked my husband what was in the package. With shrugged shoulders, he replied that he didn't know.

Upon splitting open the packing tape with the serrated kitchen knife, I began to laugh, feeling a cozy warmth spread throughout my being. Wrapped in brown paper were two individually molded plastic packages, each containing a letter opener. The openers had plain, redwood-colored ergonomic handles with non-serrated blades, measuring 8.5 inches long. Each one fit my slim hand perfectly.

One might have thought a 5-carat perfect diamond had been wrapped and given to me, which would have been a sweet surprise as well. Nevertheless, the fact that my husband of 60 years would make an effort to find the perfect letter opener to my liking was a gift in itself. He is a thoughtful person. The paper knife emotionally touched my heart and soul.

WHY CAN'T I HAVE A COOKIE?

Living geographically close to our three grandchildren in northwest New Jersey has afforded my husband and me the opportunity to be part of their lives. From their early formative years, Michael (6), Anthony (4), and Isabella (2), we were fortunate to attend various school activities and extracurricular events such as dancing, karate, baseball and basketball games, and band concerts.

Another aspect of the grandchildren's developing years was being part of their religious education. In addition to helping Michael and Anthony with their catechism assignments in preparation for receiving the Sacrament of the Holy Eucharist (also known as First Holy Communion), we also attended Sunday Mass together.

Michael and Anthony the oldest grandchildren, understood the purpose of the congregation walking up the aisle to the priest to receive the Holy Eucharist. However, through the eyes of a young child, as was the case with Isabella, the circular white wafer appeared to be a cookie.

At almost 3 years of age, Isabella, the youngest grandchild, had witnessed this ritual and expression of our faith each time we attended Mass. One summer Sunday morning, after the congregation had returned to their seats following the administration of the Eucharist, Isabella climbed onto my lap. She seemed very sad and whispered in my ear, "Grandma, why don't I get a white cookie like all the people in line do?" My immediate response was to chuckle, but instead, I just held her closer to me, thinking, How do I explain this when even adults don't fully understand the concept?

I told her that the people weren't being given cookies; the small white wafer they were receiving is a symbol of our faith.

After Mass, my grandchildren and I went to lunch, as was our usual Sunday routine. Once again, Isabella brought up the question of not receiving a "cookie." My grandsons, always patient with their little sister, attempted to explain the Eucharistic Sacrament.

Surprisingly, though understandably, they gave a basic description of what transpires during the Catholic Mass. Isabella listened to her brothers, nodded, and said, "Okay." We finished our lunch and continued on with our day.

Four years later, after two years of catechism, Isabella received her First Holy Communion. She accepted the small paper-thin white wafer, her "cookie." Though she didn't fully understand the term transubstantiation—the central tenet of the Catholic faith, which is a difficult principle for adults to comprehend as well—she participated in the ritual.

Though the years have seemed to pass by more quickly than actual time, the three grandchildren have left behind their innocent elementary school years along with the chaos of middle and high school. The two grandsons have graduated from college, are employed, and are entering grad school. Isabella is in her third year of college and plans to continue her education as well.

Each of my grandchildren has developed their unique personalities. However, the one basic trait they all share is an acceptance of others and their beliefs. I would like to think that the involvement of my husband and me influenced them in their formative years.

In retrospect, while Isabella was upset that Sunday morning many years ago because she didn't receive a cookie, it turned out to be a very warm, instructional moment — a chance to discuss an important event yet to happen in her life.

Dare to Cross the Line

Their spouses were caring, thoughtful, and loving people who would do anything for them. Nevertheless, here they were, on the brink of crossing the line. Beliefs about betraying all the sanctioned vows they had made to their partners were no longer part of their values.

The decision to choose the popular restaurant, his favorite, was a calculated move. In the quiet, private, red-lacquered room during lunch, he would be relaxed and primed for the discussion of a non-existent business strategy. The ruse was meant to lure him out of the security of his home.

Upon entering the elegant, heavily draped, secluded, chamber-like area, he saw her seated between his two brothers. To her right sat his older sibling, desperately in love with her. The youngest brother, joining the intimate group, did so merely for the thrill of witnessing the deed about to unfold.

As she rose from the table to greet her husband, he clasped her extended right hand, noticing the large, pink, pear-shaped diamond ring recently gifted to her by him. When he looked into the fiery black orbs of her eyes — the very color of her hair — every part of his body sensed what was about to occur. His stare dared her to make the move. Sliding the dagger down the inside of her dark green satin blouse sleeve, she placed it in the waiting palm of her right hand, curled her fingers around it, then lifted her arm and, with a swift forward thrust, stabbed him straight on through his abdominal flesh. Blood squirted, then gushed.

Mayhem ensued. The wife and two brothers quietly and calmly exited through the back door of the trendy bistro and into the waiting midnight-blue sedan. As they laughed and studied one another — along with the satchel on the floor — the vehicle sped away. They pondered who would be next.

SIXTY

Sixty, 60, a simple, rounded, pleasing number. In numerology when combining the energies and attributes of the numerals, 6 and 0, sixty becomes a powerful symbol.

Separated we are informed, Six, 6, is associated with responsibility, reliability and stability in life. Whereas Zero, 0, represents potential, choices and spiritual passage. As an additional benefit, Zero, 0, is known to amplify the influence of the number it appears with. In this instance, we are looking at the figure 60.

Place the 6 and 0 side by side. There it is, 60. The perfect combination as indicated by my 60 plus years of friendship with Millie.

However, the real understanding of the numeral sixty is looking at the uniting of Rosemary and Bill.

Sixty years of marriage encompassing joy, parenting, diverse opinions, support, beauty, and sadness, along with a metaphysical passage. This journey together has brought them to the celebration of their 60 th wedding anniversary.

The digits in 60 have proven to be an ideal blend for them.

www.ingramcontent.com/pod-product-compliance
Lightning Source LLC
LaVergne TN
LVHW041640070526
838199LV00052B/3473